Cont

Snoqualmie NF, WA

Become a recipe tester!

Join the MONTyBOCA Community.
What does that mean?

Receive a NEW recipe from Chef Corso.
Take it outside.
Test it.
Take a couple photos.
Share feedback.

Chef Corso edits and shares with the whole community!

www.montyboca.com/recipes/recipe-tester

The Pantry

Look beyond the tuna and mashed potato packets!

Carbs

Instant Rice
Instant Mashed Potatoes
Instant Sweet Potatoes
Rice Noodles
Ramen Noodles
Grits/Polenta/Corn Meal/Masa
Tortillas (*Flour, Corn*)
Instant Cous Cous
Pre-cooked Grain Mixes
Quinoa
Stuffing Mix
Pasta (*stick with thin or small shapes for fastest cooking*)
Bread/Rolls
Bagels

Protein

Packaged Chicken
Packaged Tuna
Beef Jerky (*hydrates surprisingly well in soups)*
Smoked Salmon
Summer Sausage
Pre-cooked Bacon
Dry Salami
Pre-cooked Chicken Sausage
Pre-cooked/Packaged Tofu
Nuts/Seeds
Peanut/Nut Butter & Powder
Chia Seeds
Freeze-dried Legumes
Chickpeas, Lentils, Pinto/Black Beans
Boca Burgers
Morningstar Farms Breakfast Sausage
Field Roast Products
Soyrizo
Other Faux Meat Options

Flavor

Spice Mixes
Salsa Packets
Gravy Mixes
Lemon/Lime
Vinegars (*apple cider, balsamic, red wine, rice*)
Sesame Oil
Soy Sauce Powder
Coconut Milk Powder
Coconut Water Powder
Asian Sauces
Hot Sauce
Condiment Packets

Veggies

Snap Peas
Broccoli
Carrots, shredded/coins
Cauliflower/Cauli Rice
Bell Peppers
Shallots
Zucchini/Yellow Squash
Baby Tomatoes
Mushrooms
Brussel Sprouts
Green Beans
And others

Don't Forget

Instant Coffee/Tea
Electrolyte Tabs/Packets
Trail Bars/Other Desserts
Other snacks, your favorite

Packing Tips & Tricks

Helpful items to make your trek a breeze!

Bags

Keep your items from rolling around your backpack. Easily pack up your ingredients and recipe with stuff sacks, packing cubes or ziplocks.

Bottles

Search the grocery store or house for some threaded, sealable options.

They will help keep the oil and soy sauce off your socks!

Campy Chop Sticks

-Find 2 fallen twigs.

-Grab your pocket knife.

-Whittle them up!

Pack It out!

The most important thing when cooking outdoors:

Always....ALWAYS pack out your trash.

Don't be a litter bug!

Smoked Salmon Breakfast Sandwiches
Snoqualmie NF, WA

Ham/Bacon, Egg & Cheese Grits
Mt. Rainier, WA

Power Chia Bomb
Channel Islands, CA

Morning Glory Bowl
Oyster Dome
Bellingham, WA

Breakfast

Snoqualmie NF, WA

Smoked Salmon & Garlic Spinach Breakfast Sandwiches

Tested by
Chef Corso

2 - 4
servings

8
ingredients

25
minutes

~8.5 oz / ~240 g
per serving +water

High Calorie

Dairy Free

Gluten Free

Low Water

8 Ingredients

◆ SPECIAL INGREDIENT	US	METRIC
Oil	4 TB	100 g
Bread/Rolls, your fav	8 slices/4	8 slices/4
Smoked Salmon	4 oz	113 g
Spinach, fresh	9 oz	227 g
Powdered Eggs ◆	4 TB	35 g
Water	4 TB	40 g
Garlic/Garlic Pwdr	2 clvs/.5 tsp	2 clvs / 3 g
Lemon	1	1
Total Weight	~2.2 lbs	~1 kg

Steps

1. **Mix** water + eggs. **Stir. Sit** 5 min
2. **TURN ON BURNER: MED HEAT**
3. **Add** 2 TB oil
4. **Toast** bread on both sides
5. While toasting, **Chop** garlic, if needed
6. When toasting done, **Add** 2 TB coconut oil
7. **Add** spinach, garlic. **Cook** 1-2 min until wilted
8. **Add** egg mixture. **Stir. Cook** 2-3 min until done
9. **Squeeze** juice of 1/2 lemon on mixture
10. **Layer** smoked salmon, egg/spinach mixture on toast

EAT & PACK IT OUT

Try with your other favorite smoked fish or add some sliced tomato or cheese!

Ham/Bacon, Egg & Cheese Grits

Tested by
guanacojockey

2
servings

6
ingredients

10
minutes

~7.5 oz / ~215 g
per serving
+water

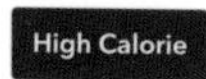

6 Ingredients

◆ SPECIAL INGREDIENT	US	METRIC
Ham/Bacon	7 oz / 3oz	200 g / 100 g
Water	12 oz	350 ml
Salt	1/2 tsp	2 g
Grits / Cornbread Mix	1/2 C	80 g
Powdered Eggs ◆	4 TB	40 g
Cheese, your fav	4 oz	100 g
Total Weight	**~1.8 lbs**	**~775 g**

Steps

1. **Chop** ham/bacon
2. **TURN ON BURNER: HIGH HEAT**
3. **Add** meat, water
4. **Boil**
5. **Add** salt, grits. **Stir**
6. **Cook** 1-2 min. **Stir**
7. **Add** cheese, extras. **Stir**

EAT & PACK IT OUT

Did you know that? It takes 21 to 45 days to cure a ham. But don't worry, it's just hangin out. Now you know!

Not a meat eater? Switch out the meat for a few veggies, greens or faux meat brekkie sausage!

Power Chia Bomb

Tested by
KB

1
servings

10
ingredients

overnight

~6 oz / ~175 g
per serving +water

Dairy Free

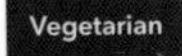

No Burner

Low Water

10 Ingredients

◆ SPECIAL INGREDIENT	US	METRIC
Water	8 oz	250 ml
Chia Seeds ◆	2 TB	16 g
Hemp Hearts or ◆ Sesame Seeds	2 TB	18 g
Flax Seed Meal ◆	2 TB	20 g
Pepitas	2 TB	16 g
Sugar/Honey Packets	2 TB / 2	25 g / 2
Coconut Milk Powder ◆	2 TB	9 g
Oil/Fat	1 TB	14 g
Dried Fruit, your fav	1/4 C	35 g
Nuts, your fav	1/4 C	35 g
Total Weight	~15 oz	~425 g

** NO COOK/NO BURNER RECIPE **

Steps

1. **Combine** all ingredients. **Stir**
2. **Sit** overnight

EAT & PACK IT OUT

Did you know that? Chia has been a building block for filling meals for centuries.
This recipe clocks in at approx:
-1100+ calories
-75 g of fat
-68 g of carbs
-31 g of protein
-17 g of fiber
+ solid levels of iron, magnesium, calcium & potassium

Morning Glory Bowl

Tested by
Minimalista

2
servings

9
ingredients

15
minutes

~5.5 oz / ~155 g
per serving
+water

High Calorie

Dairy Free

9 Ingredients

	US	METRIC
Water	8 oz	250 ml
Instant Oatmeal/Grain Mix	1 C	80 g
Brown Sugar	1-2 TB	10 g
Shredded Carrots	3 oz	70 g
Cinnamon	1 tsp	5 g
Powdered Ginger	1 tsp	5 g
Apple Sauce Cup	2 - 3 oz	110 g
Golden Raisins	1/4 C	30 g
Pecans, chopped	1/4 C	25 g
Total Weight	~1.25 lbs	~650 kg

Steps

1. **TURN ON BURNER: HIGH HEAT**
2. **Add** water, brown sugar, carrots, cinnamon, ginger, apple sauce, raisins. **Stir. Boil**
3. **Add** oatmeal
4. **TURN OFF BURNER**
5. **Stir. Sit** 5-10 min

EAT & PACK IT OUT

Did you know that? The top 4 raisin producing countries in the world are Turkey, USA, Iran and Greece. Now you know!

Panzanella
Gas Works Park
Seattle, WA

Pizza Grain Bowl
North Rim
Grand Canyon, AZ

Meat Salad - Mandarin
Redondo Beach, CA

Kale Caesar Salad
Joshua Tree NP, CA

No-Cook Lunch

North Rim - Grand Canyon, AZ

Pizza Grain Bowl

Tested by
Dirty Linda

2 - 4
servings

9
ingredients

15
minutes

~11 oz / ~325 g
per serving

High Calorie

Gluten Free

No Burner

Low Water

9 Ingredients

◆ SPECIAL INGREDIENT	US	METRIC
Quinoa or Grain Mix ◆	16 oz	500 g
precooked	or 3 1/2 C cooked	
Olive Oil	1/4 C	100 g
Lemon	1	1
Baby Tomatoes	8 oz	225 g
Pepperoni/Italian Salami	6 oz	240 g
Mozzarella/your fav cheese	4 oz	120 g
Olives	2 oz	60 g
Oregano	2 tsp	5 g
Chili Flake	1 tsp	2 g
Total Weight	~2.8 lbs	~1.3 kg

** NO COOK/NO BURNER RECIPE **

Steps

1. **Chop** salami, cheese, veggies, if needed
2. **Mix** all ingredients
3. **Sit** for 10 min

EAT & PACK IT OUT

Make this your favorite pizza! Veggie, meaty, hawaiian...go nuts!
Did you know that? Peru produces over 50% of the worlds quinoa.
Now you know!

Kale Caesar Salad

Tested by
Bellolipop

2 - 4
servings

10
ingredients

15
minutes

~4 oz / ~250 g
per serving

Gluten Free

No Burner

Low Water

10 Ingredients

	US	METRIC
Olive Oil	1/4 C	55 g
Mayo Packets	4	40 g
Dijon Mustard Packets	2	20 g
Lemon	1	1 g
Garlic Powder	1/2 tsp	2 g
Salt	1 tsp	5 g
Black Pepper	1/2 tsp	2 g
Kale	2 bunch	2 bunch
Baby Tomatoes	1 pkg/10.5 oz	300 g
Parmesan Cheese	1/4 C	25 g
Total Weight	~2 lbs	~1 kg

** NO COOK/NO BURNER RECIPE **

Steps

1. **Mix** olive oil, mayo, mustard packets, lemon juice, garlic powder, salt, black pepper.
2. **Let sit** for 5 min
3. **Chop** kale, tomatoes
4. **Mix** kale, tomatoes, parmesan cheese, dressing
5. **Sit** for 5 min

EAT & PACK IT OUT

Did you know that? California and Alaska each have eight national parks
Now you know!

Panzanella

Tested by
Satty

2 - 4
servings

10
ingredients

15
minutes

~10 oz / ~300 g
per serving

Dairy Free

Vegan

Vegetarian

Gluten Free

No Burner

Low Water

10 Ingredients

	US	METRIC
Crusty French Bread	1/2 lg loaf	1/2 lg loaf
Olive Oil	1/4 C	50 g
Red Wine Vinegar	1/4 C	50 g
Baby Tomatoes	1 pkg / 10.5 oz	300 g
Cucumber	1	1
Basil, fresh	2 TB	10 g
Artichoke Hearts	1 can (15.5 oz)	1 can (440g)
Garlic Powder	1 tsp	5 g
Salt	1 tsp	5 g
Black Pepper	1/2 tsp	2 g
Total Weight	**~2.5 lbs**	**~1.2 kg**

Steps

** NO COOK/NO BURNER RECIPE **

1. **Tear** bread into bite sized pieces
2. **Cut** tomatoes in half
3. **Chop** basil, cucumber
4. **Open** can. **Drain**
5. **Combine** all ingredients in mixing container/ziploc
6. **Mix. Sit** for 10 min

EAT & PACK IT OUT

Great with Salami or Cheese!

Meat Salad - Mandarin

Tested by
MBear

2
servings

10
ingredients

20
minutes

~9 oz / ~250 g
per serving

High Calorie

Dairy Free

No Burner

Low Water

10 Ingredients

	US	METRIC
Packaged Chicken	4-5 oz	150 g
Beef Jerky	2-3 oz	100 g
Mandarin Oranges	1-2 peeled or 1 - 4 oz cups	110 g
Carrots, coins or shredded	1/2 C	50 g
Sliced Almonds	1/4 C	25 g
Sesame Oil	1 TB	15 g
Rice Vinegar	2 TB	25 g
Soy Sauce	1-2 TB	25 g
Ginger Pwdr	1 tsp	2 g
Total Weight	~1.1 lbs	~500 g

Steps

NO COOK/ NO BURNER RECIPE

1. **Chop/Rip** meat if needed
2. **Combine** all ingredients in ziploc or mixing container
3. **Mix**
4. **Sit** for 10-15 min

EAT & PACK IT OUT

Try with some green onions, sriracha or sesame seeds!

Carbonara Pasta
Olympic NP, WA

Canada Bomb
Wallace Falls
State Park, WA

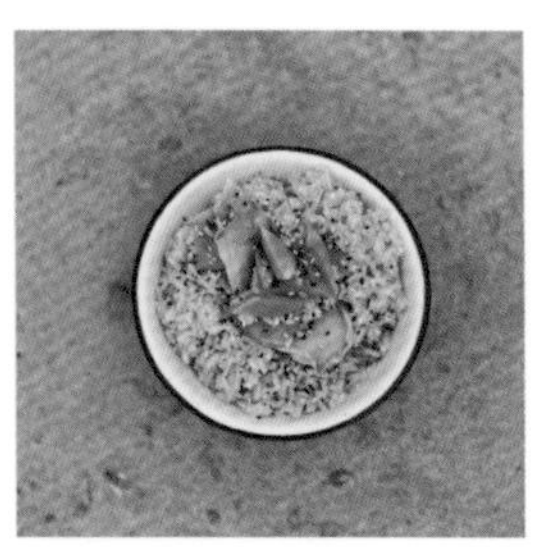

Mango Fried Rice
Hawaii Kai
Honolulu, HI

Cuban Black Bean Soup
Backwoods, WA

Dinner

Staircase - Olympic NP, WA

Carbonara Pasta

Tested by
Chef Corso

2
servings

9
ingredients

15
minutes

~7 oz / ~200 g
per serving
+water

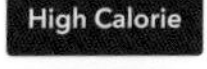

Gluten Free

9 ingredients

◆ SPECIAL INGREDIENT	US	METRIC
Water	16 oz	450 ml
Pasta	8 oz	225 g
Salt	1/2 tsp	2 g
Garlic Powder	1 tsp	5 g
Powdered Eggs ◆	4 TB	20 g
Bacon, precooked	3 oz	90 g
Parmesan Cheese	1/4 C	10 g
Mustard Packet	1	5 g
Black Pepper	1/2 tsp	2 g
Total Weight	~1.9 lbs	~850 g

Steps

1. **TURN ON BURNER: HIGH HEAT**
2. **Add** water, pasta, salt, garlic powder
3. **Cook** until pasta almost done. **Stir**
4. **Drain** water. **Reserve** 2-3 oz in pot
5. **Add** eggs, bacon, cheese, mustard, pepper. **Stir**
6. **Cook** 1-2 min

EAT & PACK IT OUT

Did you know that? Sliced bacon was first introduced in 1924 by Oscar Mayer. Made it really easy to cook up and enjoy!
Now you know!

Canada Bomb: Hashbrowns x Ramen

Tested by
megtheegg

1
servings

6
ingredients

15
minutes

~15 oz / ~400 g
per serving +water

6 ingredients

	US	METRIC
Water	12 oz	375 ml
Ramen	1 pkg / 3 oz	85 g
Beef Jerky	3 oz	85 g
Dried Hashed Browns	1 pkg/ 4.25oz	125 g
Beef Gravy Mix	1 pkg / .85 oz	25 g
White Cheese/Curds	4 oz	115 g
Total Weight	**~1.8 lbs**	**~810 g**

Steps

1. **TURN ON BURNER: HIGH HEAT**
2. **Add** water, jerky. **Boil**
3. **Add** ramen
4. **Cook** until almost done
5. **Add** hashbrowns, gravy mix. **Stir**
6. **TURN OFF BURNER**
7. **Add** cheese. **Stir**
8. **Cover. Sit** 10 min

EAT & PACK IT OUT

You can mix in the gravy or cook separately after for an extra 1-2 min.

Mango Fried Rice

Tested by
hulabutterfly

2 - 4
servings

9
ingredients

20
minutes

~7 oz / ~205 g
per serving
+water

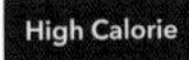

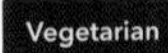

Gluten Free

9 ingredients

	US	METRIC
Water	16 oz	475 g
Instant Rice	2 C	450 g
Sesame Oil	2 TB	25 g
Soy Sauce	1/4 C	50 g
Sriracha	1 TB	10 g
Rice Vinegar	2 TB	25 g
Green Onion	1/2 bunch	1/2 bunch
Mango, fresh or dried	2 / 1 C	2 / 25 g
Garlic Powder	1/2 tsp	2 g
Total Weight	**~2.75 lbs**	**~1.3 kg**

Steps

1. **TURN ON BURNER: HIGH HEAT**
2. **Add** water. **Boil**
3. **Chop** mango, green onions, if needed
4. **Add** rice, garlic powder, mango. **Cover, Sit** for 10 min in pot
5. **TURN OFF BURNER**
6. **TURN ON BURNER: MED HEAT**
7. **Add** sesame, soy, sriracha, rice vinegar to cooked rice
8. **Cook** 3-5 min. **Stir, stir**
9. **Add** green onions
10. **Cook** 1 min

EAT & PACK IT OUT

Did you know that? Pinnacles National Park in California was designated on January 10, 2013 and is one of America's newer national parks. Now you know!

Cuban Black Bean Soup

Tested by
momjeans

2
servings

10
ingredients

15
minutes

~4.5 oz /
~125 g
per serving
+water

Dairy Free

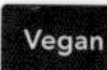

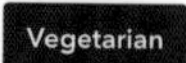

10 ingredients

◆ SPECIAL INGREDIENT	US	METRIC
Olive Oil	2 TB	25 g
Red Bell Pepper	1	1
Shallot/Dried Onion	2/1 tsp	2/5g
Garlic/Garlic Pwdr	2 clvs/1/2 tsp	2 clvs/2 g
Dehydrated Black Beans ◆	3 C	285 g
Water	24 oz	700 ml
Salt	to taste	to taste
Cumin	2 TB	10 g
Lime	1	1
Plantain Chips ◆	4 oz	113 g
Total Weight	~2.6 lbs	~1.2 kg

Steps

1. **Chop** garlic, shallot, red pepper, if needed
2. **TURN ON BURNER: MED HEAT**
3. **Add** olive oil, red pepper, shallont/onion, garlic, salt, cumin
4. **Cook** 2-3 min. **Stir**
5. **Add** water. **Boil**
6. **Add** black beans
7. **Stir. TURN OFF BURNER. Sit** 5-7 min
8. **Garnish** w/ plantain chips, lime

EAT & PACK IT OUT

Did you know that? Plantains are a good source of hearty fuel rich in potatssium, fiber and vitamin A. Now you know!

Potato Chip Bowl
Klahanie Ridge, WA

Dorito Enchilada Bowl
Toleak Point, WA Coast

Corn Nut Pork Rind Pozole
Evergreen, CO

Cheez-It Cheesy Grits
Mt. Shasta, CA

Truckstop

Klahanie Ridge - Olympic NP, WA

Potato Chip Mashed Potato Bowl

Tested by
Chef Corso

2
servings

3
ingredients

5
minutes

~4 oz /
~100 g
per serving
+water

High Calorie

Vegetarian

Gluten Free

3 ingredients

	US	METRIC
Water	16 oz	450 ml
Instant Mashed Potatoes	4 oz	113 g
Potato Chips, your fav flavor	1.5-3 oz	88 g
Total Weight	~1.5 lbs	~650 g

Steps

1. **TURN ON BURNER: MED HEAT**
2. **Add** water. **Boil**
3. **Add** mashed potatoes. **Stir**
4. **Cook** 1-2 min until done
5. **Add** crushed chips, any other extras

EAT & PACK IT OUT

Jazz this up any way you like! Cheese, green onions, broccoli, bbq chips, jalepeno, go nuts and I'm pretty sure any combo of mashed potato and chips is going to be good.

Corn Nut Pork Rind Pozole

Tested by
NomNomNate

2
servings

10
ingredients

15
minutes

~6 oz / ~175 g
per serving +water

High Calorie

Dairy Free

Gluten Free

10 ingredients

	US	METRIC
Water/Beer, lighter style	12 oz	350 ml
Corn Nuts	2 bags (3.5 oz)	100 g
Pork Rinds	1-2 oz	30-50 g
Garlic Powder	1/2 tsp	2 g
Salsa, Red	4 oz	115 g
Cilantro	1/2 bunch	1/2 bunch
Green Onions	1/2 bunch	1/2 bunch
Dried Oregano	1 tsp	2 g
Salt	to taste	to taste
Lime	1	1
Total Weight	**~1.5 lbs**	**~700 g**

Steps

1. **TURN ON BURNER: HIGH HEAT**
2. **Add** water/beer, corn nuts, pork rinds, garlic powder, salsa to pot
3. **Stir. Boil. Cook** 5-7 min
4. **Chop** cilantro, green onions
5. **Garnish** w/ cilantro, green onions, oregano, lime wedge

EAT & PACK IT OUT

Try with alllll the flavors of Corn Nuts. Could find a great new combo!

Doritos Chicken Enchilada Bowl

Tested by
Morg & Subalpinetees

2
servings

6
ingredients

15
minutes

~10 oz / ~300 g
per serving +water

High Calorie

Dairy Free

Gluten Free

Low Water

6 ingredients

	US	METRIC
Water	4 oz	115 g
Salsa, Red	1 C	200 g
Doritos, you fav	3 oz	88 g
Packaged Chicken	7 oz	285 g
Lime	1	1
Salt	to taste	to taste
Total Weight	**~1.5 lbs**	**~700 g**

Steps

1. **TURN ON BURNER: HIGH HEAT**
2. **Add** water, salsa, chicken
3. **Stir. Cook** 1-2 min
4. **Add** crushed doritos
5. **Stir. Cook** 1-2 min
6. **Squeeze** some lime

EAT & PACK IT OUT

I can't wait for all the Dorito variations on this. Cool Ranch, Verde, Sweet Chili. Bueno!

Cheez-It Cheesy Grits

Tested by
Chef Corso

2
servings

5
ingredients

10
minutes

~6 oz / ~175 g
per serving +water

Vegetarian

5 ingredients

	US	METRIC
Water	12 oz	350 ml
Grits/Polenta/Corn Bread Mix	4 oz	200 g
Cheez-Its, your fav	3 oz	90 g
Cheddar Cheese	2 oz	60 g
Salt	to taste	to taste
Total Weight	~1.5 lbs	~700 g

Steps

1. **Chop** cheese, if needed
2. **TURN ON BURNER: MED HEAT**
3. **Add** water, salt. **Boil**
4. **Add** grits/polenta. **Stir, Stir**
5. **TURN BURNER TO LOW**
6. **Stir constantly** 1-2 min until hydrated.
7. **BURNER OFF. Add** cheese. **Stir**
8. **Crush** Cheez-Its. **Add** to pot

EAT & PACK IT OUT

Did you know that? There are at least 16 flavors of Cheez-Its. Chef Corso's fav: Tabasco/Hot & Spicy. Now you know!

Fig & Pear
Balsamic Crisp
Siuslaw River, OR

Apple Cranberry
Cashew Crunch
Northeast Woods, USA

Caramelized Fruit w/
Nilla Wafer Bowl
Lynnwood Woods, WA

Caramel Apple
Kettle Corn
San Pedro, CA

Dessert

Siuslaw River - Florence, OR

Fig & Pear Balsamic Crisp

Tested by
Jew and Shiksa

2 - 4
servings

8
ingredients

20
minutes

~6 oz / ~175 g
per serving
+water

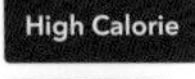

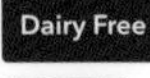

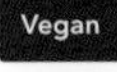

8 ingredients

	US	METRIC
Pears	2	2
Dried Figs	1 C	125 g
Water	4 oz	120 g
Brown Sugar	1/4 C	20 g
Cinnamon	1 tsp	3 g
Salt	1/2 tsp	2 g
Granola	2 C	300 g
Balsamic Vinegar	1-3 tsp	20 g
Total Weight	**~1.8 lbs**	**~820 g**

Steps

1. **Chop** pears, figs
2. **TURN ON BURNER: MED HEAT**
3. **Add** fruit, water, sugar, cinnamon, salt
4. **Stir. Cook** 5-10 min until soft
5. **Add** vinegar. Stir
6. **Add** granola on top

EAT & PACK IT OUT

Did you know that?
Fig trees have no blossoms on their branches.
The blossom is inside of the fruit.
Now you know!

Apple Cranberry Cashew Crunch

Tested by
Viper

2
servings

7
ingredients

10
minutes

~7 oz / ~205 g
per serving
+water

Dairy Free

7 ingredients

	US	METRIC
Dried Apples	1 C	80 g
Craisins	1 C	80 g
Water	8 oz	250 ml
Cinnamon	1/2 tsp	2 g
Apple Cider Vinegar	1 tsp	5 g
Kashi Crunch	1/2 C	100 g
(or other crunchy cereal)		
Cashews	1/2 C	150 g
Total Weight	~1.5 lbs	~660 g

Steps

1. **TURN ON BURNER: HIGH HEAT**
2. **Add** apples, craisins, water, cinnamon. **Stir**
3. **Cook** 3-5 min covered
4. **Chop** cashews, if you like
5. **Add** vinegar, kashi, cashews. **Stir**

EAT & PACK IT OUT

Did you know that? That texture is an extermely important component of food that is often overlooked in outdoor meals. Wet, soft foods only go so far over the long haul.
Now you know!

Caramelized Fruit w/ Nilla Wafer Bowl

Tested by
argabongo

2
servings

6
ingredients

20
minutes

~5.5 oz / ~165 g
per serving
+water

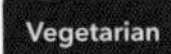

Low Water

6 ingredients

	US	METRIC
Dried Fruit 1	1/2 C	100 g
Dried Fruit 2	1/2 C	100 g
Brown Sugar	1/4 C	25 g
Water	2 oz	60 ml
Nilla Wafer, crushed	1 C	110 g
Nuts, your choice	1/4 C	25 g
Total Weight	~15 oz	~420 g

Steps

1. **Chop/Crush** nuts & Nilla wafers, as needed
2. **TURN ON BURNER: MED HEAT**
3. **Add** brown sugar, water
4. **Simmer** for 1 min
5. **Add** fruit
6. **Simmer** on **LOW** 1-2 min until caramelized
7. **Add** Nilla wafers, nuts
8. **Stir**

EAT & PACK IT OUT

Great with a nip of whiskey or rum!
Try with banana chips, raisins, dried tropical fruit, dried peaches, pears or apricots Oh My!

Caramel Apple Kettle Corn

Tested by
Chef Corso & Cosmic Crisp Apples

4 - 6
servings

5
ingredients

10
minutes

~1.3 oz / ~33 g
per serving

5 ingredients

	US	METRIC
Oil	3 TB	40 g
Popcorn	2 oz	55 g
Salt	1 tsp	5 g
Caramel	2 TB	35 g
Cosmic Crisp Apple Slices	1 apple	1 apple
Total Weight	~8 oz	~200 g

Steps
1. **Slice** apples
2. **TURN ON BURNER: HIGH HEAT**
3. **Add** oil & 3 kernels
4. **WAIT** for kernels to pop!
5. **Add** all kernels
6. **Cover. Move quick! Toss, toss**
7. When done popping, **Add** salt, caramel, slices
8. **Toss**

EAT & PACK IT OUT

Make sure to cover while you toss or you will get splattered with oil! No bueno.

VISIT US IN-STORE
stores.arcteryx.com

To enrich the quality of life for children and adults with disabilities through outdoor recreation.

www.outdoorsforall.org

Get out there...
...and COOK!

About the Chef

Chef Corso likes to eat and go outside. He's also a classically trained chef–training in Napa Valley and Northern Italy. On his treks, he noticed the food options were a little lacking. They were dry, salty, expensive and out of a bag. He started testing simple recipes, using fresh ingredients; all with the hiker/camper in mind.

The results were amazing! Tasty food that complimented the beautiful vista like nothing he had experienced before. It's his goal to share these recipes as he believes everyone should eat well on their outdoor adventures. MONTyBOCA can show you how.

Get outside. Eat well. Share the tasty experience.

While MONTyBOCA is headquartered in Seattle, Washington, all recipes are trail-tested around the world.

BocaBoca

patagonia

Text copyright 2021 by:
Steve Corson (Chef Corso) & Montana y Boca LLC
All rights reserved.
Self published in China.

Follow along:
www.montyboca.com
Instagram: @montyboca
YouTube: Chef Corso
Facebook: @elevateyourmeals
Pinterest: MONTyBOCA

Credits:
Photography: MONTyBOCA, Sattva Photography
Logo & Formatting: Ronald Viernes
Editors: Katie Cronin, Sarah Warren,
Makoto Sebuchi, Paul Stanley

First Edition - Trail Meals - Wander Edition
ISBN 978-0-578-91494-7

Get outside. Eat well. Share the tasty experience.
#elevateyourmeals
bocaboca

We are happy you're getting out there, but there is an inherent risk in taking any trip. Montaña y Boca LLC is not responsible for any personal harm or sickness experienced during your trek or while consuming food made with our recipes or suggestions.

Be mindful of your own abilities, dietary restrictions, and quality of food purchased or packed. Always pack it out, leave no trace, and cook in a safe environment to prevent forest fires. Redistribution of material is prohibited.